RARE BIRD

RARE BIRD

JAMES LUCAS

RECENT
WORK
PRESS

Rare Bird
Recent Work Press
Canberra, Australia

Copyright © James Lucas, 2021

ISBN: 9780645008913 (paperback)

 A catalogue record for this
book is available from the
National Library of Australia

Cover image: *Untitled triptych* (2002)—detail © John Wolseley, reproduced with permission.
Cover design: Recent Work Press
Set by Recent Work Press

recentworkpress.com

SS

For Sarah, Anna, and Beth

Contents

what kind of twisted ape ends up believing
the rushlight of his little human art
truer than the great sun on his back?

Don Paterson, 'Phantom'

Square Peg

I spent my twenties writing stories, trying
to wait tables. I waited tables like
Rabelais and Orwell wrote of shagging—
unconvincingly. I'd not aspired

to waiting tables. I waited tables like
Pollock juggling scotch bottle and dentist drill—
catastrophically. I'd not aspired
to moussing innocent bystanders: they watched

Pollock juggling scotch bottle and dentist drill
transfixed, as if he were intending
to mousse innocent bystanders: they dodged
lap-slop horrors that defied dry-cleaning

transfixed, as if I was intending
(as Rabelais and Orwell wrote of shagging)
to let slip horrors that defied dry-cleaning:
I spent my twenties writing stories, trying.

Karma Bin

Our fifth for dinner sits out in the dirt,
holds its voracious mouth up to receive
within the keeping of its dalek skirt
our skin and stone and core and rind and leaf
and laughter and the pip: all table traffic,
lawn and garden clippings, daily news.
There is vast acreage within this plastic
hem where dalek innards enjoy tardis views,
cook slow and, pitchfork-turned, digest
to next to nothing, crumbling loam that's dug
back into beds. Descendants of the dead
arise and our new growth is shadow tagged
and wrestled by tomato vines, the spawn
of stuff we should be done with—still reborn.

Night Waking

Against the ribcage bars of her Sing Sing
they're ringing out, my child's chestful of notes
insisting that the dark she lies in wake
to witness this the sheerest skin of time
inflating on a bellows. Then it flies.
So fly old habits of a lifetime shed,

grand plans, schedules, blown back to a shed's
unminded depths where parts unreconditioned sing
and whirr, nasal, quaint as button flies
or like old projects tagged with scribbled notes
and boxes taped-up tumbling back through time
nudged sideways by a man barely awake.

It's her pure will which trawls us in her wake.
Our old skiff's sunk, an undreamworthy shed,
its salt boards warping like a thesis in space-time.
Hers is the rigging through which salt airs sing.
For her my nets are dredging things of note:
a coral brain, jetsam abuzz with flies

abuzz with flies I start: the dreamscape flies
from our eternal trinity awake.
The breastfeed ends with child asleep, a note
(left breast or right) in mother's log, shared
body heat. And listen, mo-pokes sing
two notes two notes sown in the womb of time

where they gestate a double dream; in time
the vision I project, a far cast fly,
might snag, and jerk, hook under ribs, and sing
how dreams can flay bones bare. I lie awake.
It's six foot down, and close, the final shed.
The snuggest crib points like a post-it note.

So trepidation twists the joyful note
into Mobius strip. And many times
in the small hours when vanities are shed
it pulls hard Gs. The dream blacks out, flies
blind through chain links broken only when she wakes.
Ours is the single-sided sheet to sing.

Her few notes join our choral work. A sustained breath to fly
a kite through time. And her flesh—just awake—
I'll hold, until mine's shed, in our Sing Sing.

For John Forbes

While peaking lungs slap shut
as thin air wallets
& parquet floors resound
to confessions & to noisy fucks
you're out, reconnoitring
the package deal fringes
of paradise where dented
aspirations come to light
at carboot sales
of hawked & haggled
kits for D.I.Y. Parnassian binges
& the self-assembly funhouse
mirrors *quid pro quo* irony
(the acme of tough love)
requires, in other words
you kept your sense of humour
honest, even when you said
that poems are less important
than a mortgage & a kid.

Early Summer

With each flat hand it lifts as a blue wall
the sea becomes the sky about to fall
with—it might be—a playful smack—or pulls
—arrhythmic catch and breathing of misrule—
her legs from under her. Indifferent will
tosses her—father playing the fool—
power without mind or malice, and ecstatic
creature stirred of kelp and sand she staggers,
rights, the equal of the ocean at its worst.
Bluebottles high on the soft sand are burst
blood vessels of purely indifferent rage.
Unpausing in their leisured stroll
the great limbs of Poseidon reach this shoal
of shells, where fingers click. So breaks a wave.

Weight

'To turn to your right you lean to your left'
is nonsense to the boy whose no-good skis
propel him into that same bush again.
My father, scapegoat for frustration, sees
a boy of six can't always listen: when
he was six it made no sense—the drunken
fist, the bloodied face—but then
the boy who hears and sees has since become
the gentle man—not bully boy—who pulls
me from that bush of magnet ice. Perhaps
it's something in the way of father foils
how fateful that bush seizes on each lapse
in trust to turn advice a mishap begs
into this farce of branches catching legs.

Your chemo skull flecked like an egg
is pillow propped, your wasted arms are buckled
branches of some toppled and snow-scattered nest.
Is this the back I rode out through the break?
It breathes us in and floats us off your feet.
And I can smell your sun-oil salted back,
taste ice-cream grit, and flinch off vinyl seats
in family ovens. Kiwi Black attacks
on shoes ranked up meant Sunday afternoon,
the routine legacies of boarding house
as home, security of chores well done,
the comforts of no end left hanging loose.
So strange to see you drowse, resigned to meet
the swell come in to float you off your feet.

And now I find the ends left hanging loose
still tease and tug. It's not so much a rip
more like toes groping after sand, the loss
of purchase, spacewalk on a fraying rope:
impossible to know just what they mean,
disagreements we agreed not to resolve
in the affectionate unease of adult men.
Avoiding wounds, we missed as well the salve
of resolutions we might well have touched.
And I can't reconstruct, although I would
(reliably, like smell of sun-oiled back)
encounters past the reach of thought and word,
of intuition seeking end across a rift
like trying to turn right by leaning left.

Missing

'Does Sartre say—maybe my reading is perverse?—
love is conceiving of yourself as ideal object for
a subject you've idealised? Then love is the reverse
of the more usual duel—two looks at war
each seeking to objectify—which, in its purest form, is lust.
Sad grammar in which love and lust can't coincide
in a production on a shoestring, each of us
compelled to get by heart two less than satisfactory roles.
Or else dialogue brings together two like poles.
We inhabit the essential miss, the glancing slide.'
She turns aside, my Tutor in Philosophy
so conscious of her sunstruck arms and dress
but not in that same moment she's distracted
by my thesis and excited by my grasp
of nothingness and being—Sartre says. But this is fantasy.
It's the local understudy to Antonio Banderas
whose op-shop loafers trip after her Docs
and rattle up the gantries way over our heads
beyond the canted gods out on the tiles,
past whitewash windows, panes afloat on lead.
Deaf to the moon's bright unoriginal reply.
Blind to that grubby *Titleist* on a better lie.

We catch up for a beer. Three years have passed.
He doesn't know or care what Sartre said.
He shouts a round. He never took that class.
My smile unfixes from a mirrored mug.
I'll have to make us up inside my head.

Banksia

it stands about in dry sand unimpressed
and mum to its own boom mike spike its thousand flower heads
a whitlam era grant idea of blue-collar insouciance
its industry is folded arms and cubing squares
its shoulder shrug less shrub than pub recidivist its wreck
is asymmetric architecturally it loves to
cock its snook at burn mark fruit in candelabra
knocked up in a railway shed it has no mythological pretence
it found its umpteenth summer dull
and never had an old regret
its only Lit is births and marriages and deaths
its citizenship boats turned back and its blunt leaves
orthotic soles for gammy-legged woodchoppers so stead
y on the cooling tower plank step dodging edgy hooks.

Rock Platform, Long Reef

A sea cucumber flattens on the palm
seeming to leak and deliquesce much as
its namesake long forgotten in the fridge.
A lady finger fatter than its sheath.
And look, a liver-spotted hand is pouring
unsegmented worm. Photophobic chitons
with sharp tongues, the volunteer explains,
rasp algae from dark undersides of rocks.
His eyebrows sweep to outer peaks
pronounced as Billy Bibbit's
in the film version of Dune,
orange as the bristles of the fireworm.
Sea-star stomachs will extrude to prise apart
with unrelenting pressure stronger bivalves.
See Aristotle's lantern is tooth-plated
mouth to the sea urchin's maw,
and from the rock pools of Stagira
to the planet *Dune* is thinnest schist.
See where the chiton rasped
through undreamt eons prior to the shell midden.
And see today a white-faced heron balancing
its spear-gun head begins to swizzle stick
a rock pool with one foot. And after lunch
see surfers fight or fly up their capped plume.

At Western Plains

When siamang gibbons sing to hold their ground
an air-tight pouch vibrates beneath each chin.
Upright primates gather, marvel at the sound

and over-acted gestures. Rounded mouths
shape reverb like a didge's barking din.
When siamang gibbons sing to hold their ground

one sprints a rope bridge, scales a tree, a bough
so high and so improbably thin
upright primates, three deep, marvel at the sound

and swing bravado of this acrobatic clown
and they applaud. A young boy cries, "Again!"
When siamang gibbons sing to hold their ground

the display's recurring, urgent, loud
that in the wild occurs just daily, after dawn.
Upright primates gather, marvel at the sound

and crowd the moat three deep as vain apes bound
to stand guard every hour of the sun
when siamang gibbons sing to hold their ground.
Upright primates gather, marvel at the sound.

Darlinghurst Rd

Fruit machines accept all cards for every punter
there's an addict doorframed, they punctuate the street
as in a Florence gallery when restorers airbrush out
aureole and child to foreground areolae puckered
for remedial teething, too pure or too stoned
for lewdness, this Beatrice-free opening
whose proven images are made not marred by copywriters'
truant and genius ink! And now commercial artists
bring the day to consciousness or coffee, at least sunlight
coaxes brown meniscus eyes that swill in time to waiters' hips
which anchor-leg a relayed pilgrimage from Kenya,
scent of Africa upmarket from shorestruck sailors
whose sleeveworn hearts are just the boon
a plein-air florist needs: her birthmark
ups the stakes: should I tell you what she feels?
Or say a foil of jaywalk zebras plead panache
as if their skin complaint might be the next hot topic
for homeopaths? That kills the conversation
since you can't fit them on the side of a bus, or the back of a cab.

Sydney

Three UK years & a day long haul
to hear it strange: the Heathrow tongue
stretched flat at Kingsford Smith
desiccated as Mascot lawns look:
fruit coughed up in declare it for Australia
quarantine stalls recompressing feet
lop-sided on an interrogative lilt
& customs explanations don't sound
pat—I'm through arrivals, the turnout
mambo in fruitsalad & lorikeet as if
history stops with carnivale & the state casino;
or sensing a poem here has to include bingo
jism & guilt; that it should clear a throat
colloquial as currawongs: their call

Cheap eat café hairs of the dog
the beach takes a Bunsen
to eyestrain sand, crinklecut, whitehot
as bondi glamorama crewcuts
do sushi: I didn't inhale,
watched skaters blade the promenade
backed by spraycan art & overlooking
a kilometre of lightly salted
skins we're delicious! Can I sting you
to wet the other, bright as a diamante
navel stud front reflecting at speed?
How mindful of self-aware, critical spins
on body-piercing we culminated nowhere
near the un'important' water, avoided junk.

Did flying south outstrip the blue pencil
granted we're easy with an either-handed grip
being unrapped? Anything goes local style
in your face as Parramatta Road billboards
that's the myth, struthious as gritted teeth
& eyes from wound-down windows. A '68
careers not past being drugfucked from the zoo
at western plains, they're culling private demons,
angels had it with petrol fumes. Sirens
squeal at lanehog rush approaches to
the Cahill's obligatory harbourscape:
at its fore & aft juncture less like sails than
buttocks rising from a fussy hem, operatic
prelude to dunk me, take me brash.

Short Story

Nudge-butt commuters on the citylink
all domino another yard. The merits
of batting first on a 'Gabba greentop leave
something to mull over in the jam
of traffic merging for the Harbour Bridge
as batsmen must work hard for every run.

Car radio's a god-send on this run.
An on-air risqué joke provides a link
to his mistake: can he uncross that bridge?
As if to prove selections are on merit
Clarke keeps a yorker out with downward jam
but hurts his back: next ball's outside off, a leave.

The driver cannot wait to go on leave.
Each day he plans to take a morning run
and then relax over croissants with jam,
pass hours in torpor like a missing link;
at least a man on holiday from merit
can devote himself to cricket and to bridge.

But two and two make up a four for bridge
and even now his wife has packed to leave.
She's had it with the spurns that patient merit
takes of worthy bores, she's on the run
to an old flame (he never made the link):
She thinks she's getting his money for jam.

It saddens her to leave him in this jam
but there is now a gulf she cannot bridge.
Last birthday they spoke only via a link:
he was at a conference, couldn't leave.
His back means he won't take the dog for runs.
The family lawyer says her case has merit.

And though he's fully conscious of his merit
(as he nips smoothly through the easing jam
Clarke gets his fifty with a cheeky run)
he knows it's up to him to build a bridge
to the wife he's now decided not to leave:
she'll get the necklace; he'll add extra links.

So the sestina's merit is to bridge
the tempting fruit and sticky jam, when asking no-one's leave
events and heroes run through fated links.

The Way That We Read Europeans

Cobbled round a fountain I was pushing through a tide
of rising pigeons to a café table where a burgher sipping
reused grounds was toying with a stale biscotti, definitively
old-world every inch the actor and inspiring confidence

he could deliver on the script. On cue out of nowhere
sliding through the flower-stall a vespa stalled, coughing up
a gravelburnt stand-in for the anarchist, the old man's nephew.
To be honest their dialogue lacked zip. We were trying

to recall the café patrons' faces from the dentist's *Paris Match*,
scanning newsstands stocked with month-old papers. Headlines
said the nephew had absconded with a self-described actress:
well-shod we thought but too inclined to dunk her biscuit?

That first evening she'd play dutiful niece, preparing supper
for a screening of the daily rushes, not knowing the subtitling
team's absence meant that nothing could be eaten.
Guest-stars predictably threw tantrums. In the end the project

was re-jigged as travelogue art history. Locations found
a chapel with an ossuary lending trinket glass a gravitas.
We wouldn't buy it. We wanted to go back to the old man
at the café, argued that the vespa crash had never happened.

We didn't like him as the bookish pedant, wanted him
descending without interruption in a lineage from village craftsmen.
Or we'd compromise, accept him as a po-faced ferry captain
living off his contraband, freeing the odd dissident.

But we demanded that the niece be genuine, a stranger
to bordellos, her rise to elegance beyond recriminations.
We wanted their faces effortlessly to assume the anguish
and refinement that we'd seen first hand in black and

white TV ads that sell Melbourne as our European city.

All Day Dusk

Dressed in topsoils dumped from windblown farms
cars formed up in the station parking lot
are terracotta warriors in a just-opened tomb

furred in the dusk of 8 am.
A citybound commuter coughs over his paper's
front page photo of a golfer silhouetted

on paprika sky, his swung iron aloft
a Huey rotor pitched too far, about to kiss the ground
and fireball. Today's lead story quotes the PM's

smoke-affected vision: now is not the time
for climate talk. Beyond the sealed window
orange tongues of day are rust marks

licking playing fields white as enamel,
reaching for a mouth that plugs
rebreathed air behind its mask

as if plugging doors with towels did more than slow
our progress to the equilibrium of stinking hair,
tight lungs, or cleansed the stale and bitter haze

from streets like hessian sacks, while inside
no-one's checking batteries, no-one hears
the radio advising that it's now too late to leave.

Jazz

Dissonance
(if you are interested)
leads to discovery

William Carlos Williams, *Paterson*, Book Four

i.

a flying sax
converses with
a sedentary piano,

feeling
for a quickness
under pressure

then ascending
flights of basement stairs
without a landing

ii.

because it's
neither old
nor masterly
this life that's still
haphazardly

making planes
and volumes out
of incognito
coffee cups
and newspapers

and through
the shutters,
                    kites

iii.

and later, stars
remote above
gutter detritus.

the skyline
is a skin hocked
to tattooists,

inking
the fixed intervals
of neon signage.

the subtext is
the fullsleeve cartoon
of a biker.

iv.

and walls ruined by damp
said Leonardo in his notebooks
may suggest the contours
of heroic landscapes

as a mattress in an alley
strikes a lithe pose stately
as a Henry Moore,
basking in adoring glances

off surrounding bottle glass,
the eyes of Latin lovers.

v.

following the cue-ball
slowing to the corner pocket

(brinkmanship of early openers)

because yes,
we've a sense of blindness
that attends our every enterprise

and is itself attentive,

I'm thinking of Thoreau
and Frank O'Hara

navigating margins wasting paper

vi.

a phrase thrown off the keyboard
caught within the cornet's
chamber:

summertime: the pollinators
drowse between fortuitous
encounters with impromptu
nectar

(remember when you heard
the bee trapped in the can of
cola?)

vii.

admit it:
no this isn't
flu, it's love

and hope

is the proboscis
dipping

or at worst
a petrol pump

reholstered
in its bowser.

viii.

the forest is all char
and luminescent
shoot, no branch:
leaves are furring
every blackened trunk
fluorescent lime,
and through
this dichromatic,
vistas, formerly invisible:
the foreground
frames a caravan,
blackened as a campfire tin:
now close in:
Django's melted hand is
reinventing jazz guitar

ix.

it seems inevitable, this music
abruptly flinging itself forward
mind and into darkness
wresting order from disorder
giving birth to and destroying:

like the indrawn breath and exhalation
of a woman in sky-blue running
backwards, waving, when
a man in blue serge

turns the corner whistling

The Necklace

1. de Maupassant

Petty bourgeois who count their sous
will hanker after vanities
so invitations to a ball
gilt-edged are subtle cruelties:
without a dress she can't attend
so stays at home, dies of despair—
or borrows from a patron friend
a gown, a choker she can wear
that's torn, that's lost (so children drop
always off-limit precious things).
Found in austere palatial shops
replacements bought on credit bring
on debt's unflinching wrestle hold:
she scrubs, she launders, she is old.

2. *Zola*

A man of paper fortune debt makes reckless
about his wife's bankrupted neck lets fall
(the bill unpaid) a keenly-rumoured necklace
then hosts the season's most outlandish ball.
His creditors see all is well, and lend.
His thirst for cash an all-consuming thirst
is of one kind; the peasant who abets
for plots of land her sister's rape drinks earth;
a maiden parched for love derails the train,
makes carriages play leapfrog in the snow;
one hot for justice dynamites a mine.
For now the author lets the lovers go.
Their feet stomp hands that grasp the lower rung
for they are both immortal, being young.

Lyrebird

We've come into the forest late
or it seems late—for want of light—
but there is music in this wood:
the tramp jacket dun lyrebird
whose throat for a blind orchestra
is the black pit, tight aperture
lyrebird acoustics magnify.
Not *liar* as in *telling lies*

as children think: it may be years
before we see the knee-propped lyres
on old vases in picture books,
slip round the side, beat from some nook
name nested in subconsciousness.
We see the tail, its forward thrust.
We hear the love songs on a loop
of samples, scratched, enlarge the scope

of simple tunes in hero riffs
and trills of a compulsive thief
tripped like delinquent car alarms
in chop-shop rebirths where the lyre's
a front, a flourish to distract
so dull leaves raked and feather-wrapped
can parrot what the bright birds skite:
Is that my song's extent? Not quite:

I scratch around to remix in
intent and phrasing of my own:
the bridge from cry to mating call,
from serenade to power tool.
And should you cut through oilskin
dissect the vocal cords and brain
the innards spread defy you, mute,
give nothing up the echo throat

that catches in a quicksand pull
the log camp, white noise, urban sprawl
along with crow and lark and crake.
I hear. I swallow. Take the bait.
I'm not, despite the double bluffs
of lyre, a liar after all.
I sound all ams, mouth all your ifs.
You're just one more ventriloquist.

The Garden

With threaded beads of rain the spiderwebs
raise arch on vaulted arch of eyebrow studs
(say 'garland fairy lights' to please the mob),
the micro-metallurgist at each hub
extruding a St Andrew's cross long-limbed
awaiting prey vibration of its net,
the planes at angles variously trimmed
and layered for a polaroid effect
of integrated air traffic control.
Their tick-plump cousins fatten in the eaves
on flies tucked into cotton cobweb folds
old gauze unravelled like a bandage sleeve,
unsightly yes but what annoys the eye
fly-proofs the house. Unless I am the fly.

Loom

A staple. A romantic trope.
The lovers' fingers interlock.
But try it—awkward knuckle squeeze
unjoints soft-knocking carnal hope.

So evening, morning, week by week,
weave onto hangers dress and shirt,
weave mattress mesh to bear our weight.
So make the bed to fit the sheet.

And when the dreaming's long and good
weave grapevine through the trellises
weave salt and pepper through a tress
weave winter nests of kindling wood

weave branches through the fire and milk,
red maple leaves into the lawn,
and raise the count of thread per inch
in fabric tough and sheer as silk.
A house pitched steady as a tent.

Milk

1.

the blotters dairy cattle make.
pianos melted. write a score.

2.

lining throats
with August sleet
in mid-December

3.

beneath twenty snowy peaks
twenty cappuccinos

4.

you say I lack the milk
of human kindness.
I give you the empty carton

5.

the half-drunk tumbler's
second skin.
the absolutely ordinary
halo at the bottleneck.

Pandora

If I could fix upon the slightest thing
I'd choose a moment breakfasting with Beth
when we discuss the kookaburra's song

a good hour earlier, that woke us both.
That pre-dawn larrikin has fallen quiet
and passed to us possession of the earth

so that this day, hold what it might,
balloon glass that I'm turning by the stem
is fattened to the brim with light

swilled in to flush out the stale lees of dream.
This is the hour Beth tells me of her world.
'Dadda,' she asks, 'Do you know...' And so begins

an inventory of things I must be told:
three reasons why the best colour is brown
how frogs are born of origami folds

how concertina maps make flattened ground
and how the earth used not to be so big
that's why the older bones are deeper down:

phenomena that I could not predict
make all her globe. Its sliding plates are stocked
with phyla taxonomically adrift

from mine so our conversing picks the locks
of what I had assumed the slightest things.
Cut sandwiches are airlocked in a box.

We're ready. She unclips the lid. Looks in.

Show and Tell and News

A must-see wonder on the walk to school
      Beth shows me where the lizard makes its home
a concrete paver lifted half an inch
      off true, most likely on a root, so it won't fall.
She gets down low on both knees and looks in,
      as these things must be done, of course they must:
a child on all fours breathes into a vent
      through slabs off-balance, through frett metal nests
of deranged ikebana, fug and dust,
      and she is blood-badged, no older than Beth
who spots white cockatoos against the blue
      beheading native flowers for their seeds.
Talc powdered clowns stare still in disbelief
      through their foundations razed, these ghosts
who people rubble of regimes—regimes
      don't fall, not to the naked mind
that must hook under pavers half an inch.
      Safe haven for a liquid metal skink.
A gap to madden local dogs. They're teased
      like rescue dogs she'll learn about in school.

Rhyme

A half good reason looking for a rhyme
might say *because it's there*, or else *I do*,
a soundbite that convinces on a whim.

Agnostics, theists, tone-deaf sceptics find
if something resonates it must be true.
A half good reason looking for a rhyme

wants jingles pitched to flatter its best side,
wants drumming hooves conjured from tubs of glue.
A soundbite that convinces on a whim

is chewing wax. It is the earworm inside
pink cathedrals where echoes confuse
a half good reason looking for a rhyme,

where mumbling dreams prise open eyes
of demagogues who slept safe in their tombs.
Soundbitten, they bring rigour to a whim.

Wake up! The hammer strikes. The anvil chimes.
The stirrup jangles. Heralds bring the news
of half good reason having found a rhyme.
The soundbite. The hot lamp. Luminous skin.

The Lookout Tree

Stonemasons who raised Notre Dame knew how
clean verticals inspire, how high-thrust trunks
make open sky of steep-pitched wood.
Better this karri, Gloucester Tree, one-ninety feet
and regal among dukes if not for Gaudi's touch,
the spiral ladder of embedded rods which screws up
to an eyrie. A lookout tree once used for spotting fires.
For tourists now. You feel steel flexing on the outer rim
of thin rungs not, in truth, two feet apart, ascending
anti-clockwise as if abetting a right-handed siege,
as if the architect of castle keeps had flipped.
Not me. I take my time. A second for each rung.
The tree's a backwards-tripping clock whose spring I wind
tight enough for goosebumps, high enough to catch
the pig-grunt gears and understand the klaxon in my head
is chainsaws heard across a half-mile twenty years.
Above that sound now, in its stead a hawk and spitting
crosscut saw grasped either end by dripping men.
Their tree set on its hinge, they work the felling cut.
I look down on the thick and thinning crowns
of their bare heads. Escaping its wrecked cage
the air looks up, while I look flat into a distance,
see a rubbed chalk line of cloud that isn't cloud,
heat shimmer in one patch of sky.
The moment comes to rest, expands, then clamps
as do my hands, my throat, and the dumb
tethered horses underneath me shift and shake their heads
but don't, or won't, or maybe can't look up.

For Squirrel Nutkin

Less question mark—to high sheen tile affixed—
than cursive *e* or lazy ampersand
synecdoche for Valentino cowlick
a curlicue *sans* character, one strand
or, grooving off a hairbreadth nib, black ink:
the miracle of how its end was met
above the *pissoir*—rafting on the stink?—
less jaw dropping than Teller and Penn
nevertheless must give us pause
we might reflect on thus: less than a word
aquiver shoots us back to the first cause
of each updraughting spiral whirlybird—
here's *obiter* to Adam's downstroke I,
the name he signed himself on the first day.

Dinner with Patrick White

It is the flesh that mortifies the soul.
It is the body that condemns
each sortie from slow-starving
keep to failure. Outside are lawns

too long to mow. Unheimlich hoists
rotate to trip club-footed angels.
Milk upon the kitchen hob grows skin
and other risible complexions

putty-fill the bones whose veils
must shift and tic—their sober task
to spot amidst the ripeness that thing
turning in the fruitbowl's oval glass.

Aubade

We've neither nightingale nor lark
to wake us yet we're not alone:
hydraulic sighs of council trucks
speak empathetically of dawn.

Their arms extended draw the arc
of vessels, flown and emptied, down
to dismounts that we aim to stick
but rattle. And the work moves on.

The balance that the spent regain
is in rank ballast, on the mark
where every skybound surge begins.
Under the lid and in the dark.

Breakfast with Pablo Neruda

would have to include eggs,
an armful the gum
-booted rooster
pulled from dirty
snow flurries,
skin-toned beneath
feather flake
and faecal spot
full moons grown heavy
wide-hipped
bearing suns
that whisper *yes*! again *yes*!
on the pan's iron lip
                        as dawn
leapfrogs the windowsill
and thickening whites
hide one rogue shard
there would be glass
-less sightlines
to wire mesh
standing proud
light feathers of
a hundred sun-spear
palisade, the cage,
the pueblo, Pablo's coop.

Fifty

They step through to the surface, drawn by light,
more ghosts exposed and adding to the stock
of negatives. Kept under key and lock
through decades the tinned spools accumulate.
Like Clark Gable and Leigh in *Casablanca*
suave as DiCaprio as Charlie Kane
one spool wraps tight the rushes where an actor
eternal youth who'll never make her name
got her big break in *My Brilliant Career*.
The headline parts no poster ever billed
and Oscar-winning roles that never played
press hard against vault ceilings, steal the air
from breathless selves—those critics who can't cruel
nor laud the greatest movies never made.

Tomorrow

I'm here. It's just a dream. And it can't hurt
I tell you, shaken dreamer in the night.
I don't explain the things I would avert
are deaf to words and unafraid of light,
the keening drone, prayerfully severed head,
and ribs cracked in the crush for blockade crumbs.
Things you don't see before you go to bed.
The globe you see is marked with grubby thumbs
(it's not a toy don't spin) clear oceans, continents.
Viewed from astride our cushion elephants
we can agree that animals are friends
and find their actual imagined lands
and pore over the globe you can't help spin
and watch tomorrow and tomorrow striding in.

Holiday Snaps

1.

Monaro sky yellow
as the hills it sponges
promised kisses—heavy rain.

2.

fumbling for yesterday's
donut (narrowly missing
last night's roadkill).

3.

black crow feather underfoot,
overhead the cirrus
skeletons of fish.

4.

sheep tussock above
shallow tarns. In reception
there's a cup of stale tea.

5.

gibber flint summit
with flower pinheads
focus: five white petals.

6.

cricket on the wireless
only interferes with static
whine from burning woodsap.

Gunlom

The first rule is avoid the ants. The second: pitch for shade.
Sync your tent with the gums' thin-limbed predatory gait.
We know this campground capsized in the Wet:
floodmarks stain the toilet block. We've heard
mature males seek new territory as the waters drop.
So while the plungepool beckons like a mineral seam
the bank in my mind hides a larder crammed with meat.
He's there in boardies waterhole wet, his paunch a leather
bumbag, a Territorian he says but not he says a *local* local.
All smiles he's insistent everyone including kids must swim
right *here*, below the falls. The Parks sign won't commit.
The path up to the other, safer pool is in full sun
and it's a million years since last it rained.
Though he's indulgent of my idiocy (haven't I spoken so
to British backpackers of sharks?) my steely courtesy
is judged a snub to his damp manliness. I see I've botched
my entry to the apex club. His eyes are humourless
as a thermomix enthusiast invested in a pyramid scheme.
And dark comes quickly, with it bonfires, alarm glass.
I make out micro bats, ink flecked over dusk, two flecks,
three, the slipped disks of imperfect spirographs,
circuits of continuous feeding. And once turned in
what seems imagination tickling my scalp
will prove by torchlight really to be ants
thrummed to the surface by unsleeping generators.
The bats' metallic pulse I'll take on trust, as I will
all outside my hearing range, and all locations
echo sensed, off plan, and every place the ants seep.

Emuford to Lithgow

after Arthur Streeton's 'Fire's On'

I want to call the mountains *blue*
by skipping to the end of what I can't
yet read, an orange bluff that twists

a landscape into portrait mode.
I crick my neck, duckfoot my feet,
arrest the slide and face the sun
that punches through

the gap under the painter's armpit.
I need to look inside the tunnel,
taste the dust that nags
like an authentic phrase, pricks like a cough.

I need to look inside the paintbox
smutted as a lung to see the cobalt,
burnt sienna, exhale clay
in a parched gust. I need to see off

heat-struck gums shimmering
and bored with scribble, gestural now
and gaining speed I need to see

train windows flick a catalogue to feel
I'm animated air-conditioned
whistle wet with spit sufficient

to pronounce
            here Streeton's
drilling eye and loaded brush
are keen as steel
                in my best

wheezy Robert Hughes
                as if
reciting my bit part in a dys
-lexic tantrum sprung from dyn
-amite's exactly measured fuse.

More or Less

When campfires seeding spuds too hot to grip
give way to grid-drain paraphernalia
of trailer kitchenettes then luxury has tipped
over into shanty town suburbia.
The sites shrink as proliferating toys
make every lot the crazy neighbour
hoarder's: bikes sporting goods the noise
in narrow cul-de-sacs that test off-roader
skills of dads, cajoling vans
through Landcruiser dressage. Running motors
drown out surf, cool the fridges cooling cans
that dull the itch of cossie lining sand quotas.
A dune-whip wind is muted by doof-doof.
We pull stars through antennae on the roof.

Visitation, Hay Plains

Like winking Aphrodites in a file
the liquid trucks and cars solidify.
John Deere scratching dirt lifts a mare's tail.
There's tinsel at the station gates where snow
-men stand as stacks of whitewashed tyres
while Santas atop bales, lethargic, know
the slouched repose of merrily stuffed Guys.
A shredded tyre that sits up lizard like
on verges of received taxonomies
counts off sheet metal reindeer in our wake
that shimmer take flight then float down to greet
each driver, making good time, having found
a swim lane where clear water becomes clay,
the moving point where vision kisses ground.

Rare Bird

for John Wolseley

A vagrant thought to which I cannot fix a word
speaks of the soul—too big a stretch?—of search
through properties, blind chases where I catch
a bar of red, white brow or whistled note
enough for just a rapid notebook sketch
from memory that's needing working up
later, in meticulous elsewheres:
full line-ups of exhibits laid on sides
lie like embedded misquotation marks
exponentially removed, in cabinet drawers,
from airborne seeds of snow or singeing fires.
White gloves discreetly push their silence shut
not worrying a quarry only dreamt.
But Wolseley's sweep of paper barely scratched
through cover where both fire and eye have paused
grants both the hunted and the hunter room to move
a vagrant meditation without close
(that bird I thought I saw being long gone)

Thaw

Ice loaf and fished by air makes snow.
It forms as mathematic curve,

as spinnaker in dropping breeze.
Climb on your fishscales. Weight them, bite

the ice beneath an ice screw trunk
that crooks a bent finger of shade,

an icedial leaning from the sun.
All is soundless. You're the pin

-point taking up no space, pure light.
Get lost out here and you might freeze.

Indifferently you think of this.
What makes you nervous is the thaw,

the foetid soak beneath the sheen,
the bruise that hides a watercourse.

You think of your ungainliness
and of the snow bridge where the span

you hope of ski will dissipate
your weight aloft on crystal seeds,

where snow you hope full nine-tenths
air will hold up your ten stones.

At Times the Fool

Act I

Each avalanche a cracking cannon peals
off face off face: a sudden climber stands
a wool and leather apparition, steel-
-a-pied, a gloveless and frost-blackened hand
that beckons: time now for the summit push.
I draw my hood in sphincter-tight
sense rivets shearing folded in the crush
of Base Camp cots collapsing under weight
of one-hump trysts. I can't climb, can't forget.
Cold in the mountain's pit-bull bite
I watch his progress up summit arête
til bottled gas, asthmatic, gauge at nought,
whispers 'Adieu'. A lamp blinks from afar.
And black flesh thaws into a sticky tar.

Act II

Coaxed into harness by a pretty ruse
(a black-tie do of double threaded straps),
now pack-hauled, now rappelling through diffuse
refracting blue-end spectra of seracs
that tumble into labyrinth: my fate
when mask and mirror smiling both invite
me to an après rescue tête-a-tête
is downing defrost fritz, rank hams, cheap white
quaffed with chameleon's black-gartered dish:
ethereal bait. I know that her old man's
a (loaded) prick: his podcast cameras fish
the slipways where her skirts admit my hand
well-read and weasel-keen. Lust won't postpone
what pretty braille must come to. Dust and bone.

Act III

To be or not: the forced choice tests a World
Cup TV tipster octopus savant
whose jelly-eel-jarred tentacles, unfurled,
rake all the chips on everything I want.
To stake anything less is cause for shame:
that's how it looks to earnest post-pubescents
who've not yet learnt to play spread-betting games
nor realised a timely detumescence
on reflection rescued many a career.
Let those bad habits (not offences rank)
lie quiet in the closet til New Year.
Squid knot and gender in the belly's tank.
Antacid therapists arrive too late
for ersatz guts upchucking sticky fates.

Act IV

There's fun in the insanity defence
expelling from the alimentary tract
the poison, poisoner, and all pretence
of fealty or advantageous pact;
it's fun to coach them into sewing seams
of fashion boxer jocks with charge and nails;
less fun to wring the bloody mop, hear sung
the bucket-rattling airs of love's travails.
Just so, just at the point I've drunk my fill
as *auteur* of a feted splatter-flick,
less sated rivals nose the gory swill,
keen to reshoot with extra extras, tricks
like marching over eggshells. Nothing faked.
Lime lights on the mass grave that honour stakes.

Act V

If there were unions that we thought to bless
that folly died along with mountaineers
whose summit glories we could only guess:
here the terrain's flat as neglected beers
and gamers, easily exposed, clutch tight
their sleeping bags in bus shelters, their craft
and guile redundant in our bitter night:
borne high on pills or sunk in cloudy rafts
the great souls, lovers, and Machiavels
all drool-mouthed, denture-gummed, cannot repent:
so easy in-flight listening Lets it Be,
the Boeing's imperceptible descent.
Our ice-floss windows drip no curséd stars,
just rimey dross of Copen-Haagen-Daaz.

Oval Office Drinks

Zero proof is skid proof smear proof crease proof
stain proof fade proof shrink proof shower proof

30 proof is tangle proof tamper proof & rabbit proof
galley proof spark proof wind proof scratch proof

60 proof is rip proof spore proof, kid proof
rust proof shock proof grease proof & heat proof

90 proof is fool proof shatter proof sound proof
flame proof water proof & puncture proof

120 proof is bomb proof shark proof doubt proof
fire proof, leak proof, deal & appeal proof

150 proof is nuke proof, terror proof, drought proof,
stormy proof, recession proof, election proof, disease proof

180 proof is future proof, history proof, oven proof.
Proof proof. Bullet proof. Over proof.

Pitch Map

It's me who sets the field in bird's eye view
an oval on a flyleaf pencilled neat
to map arcane nomenclature for you.
The leg and off. The silly, fine and deep.
You're wanting, Anna, to know who goes where:
whose arm and loping stride make two of three,
whose reflexes trap dot balls on the square.
We draw this splendid fiction in which each
is granted place and purpose: so my sky
of glass eyes, marbles clacking in a sack
might come to seem symphonic; you might try
to chart uncounted blazes in the dark.
For now imagine pickets round a park,
a wagon wheel, the pitch where you can land
your palm and brace for cartwheels off one hand.

Scroll

the flights and gates are scrolling up the screens
the sniffer dogs pace either bank of sky
there's thermal guns, pockets patted clean
as travellers step through the gates of π

the sniffer dogs pace either bank of sky
a flight is never cancelled, just delayed
as travellers step through the gates of π
the numbers scroll the coins drop in the tray

a flight is never cancelled, just delayed
however many switchbacks in the queue
the numbers scroll the coins drop in the tray
here every tax and levy will fall due

however many switchbacks in the queue
there's thermal guns, pockets patted clean
here every tax and levy will fall due
the flights and gates are scrolling up the screens.

Sentence

There's a note by the phone says your father's dead.
The note caught her eye as she passed through the hall.
There's something she needs to get straight in her head.

The dead won't lie still. Last words are unsaid.
The battery recharges. The full hit appalls.
There's a note by the phone says your father's dead.

The pall is dissolving: unravelled thread.
The knock at the door is another cold call.
There's something she needs to get straight in her head.

I don't trust that doctor. Lies I've been fed.
Has something been stolen? Then she finds the scrawl.
There's a note by the phone says your father's dead.

A sentence in limbo, read and reread.
Annoyance. Bemusement. Vertigo. Fall.
There's something she needs to get straight in her head.

I'm just over-tired and must go to bed.
I'm sure that it's nothing. I'm sorry to call.
Your old mother's getting things straight in her head.
There's a note by the phone says your father's dead.

Song of Innocence

Thrown often by the measured
airing of deluded views

I know full well an easy tone
best serves an inane premise,

and hence my poem 'The Smiths'
(which in a draft invoked Winston

and Joan of Arc, but is at heart
about the cricketer and poet

Stevie) kicks back here, accept
-ing everymanic foot each

tic and fidget like a jockey shy
as our dood bog and baggy

may technically be green, and yet
from where I sit, beyond the palings

with the cognoscenti, I'd say even
on debut you loved to lark, waived

the egg and bacon, scuffed the Duke,
that even in the long shadow

of stumps that toe-crush gloaming
facing either end the rested, raging

John and C P Snow, spit-honed
hostilities fizzing about the ears

von richthofening dreams of
rapprochement, you, Stevie, at least

can build again from zero, turn your creams
here at the crease. You scratch your mark.

Chapel, Port Arthur

This is how god's house is loaded:
in tiered pews, screens on hinges
fourth walling each stand-up coffin.
Blinkered stalls. An ammo box.
Open mouth with every tooth pulled.

This is how god's word is spoken:
into silence. Not a whistle.
No cat either. Star bright clamour
is the bucket's empty promise.
Even the guards' shoes wear sack-cloth.

This is how the charm is broken,
this is how the lock is picked:
something catching in the voicebox
locked inside the model prison
locked to the coast of Van Diemen's

Land locked by a line of dogs;
on the dead isle in the harbour
that key scrapes, and jigs, and rattles.
On that isle the unmarked stones
are open doors. Home is the North.

They open south.

Road Bridge to the Isle of Skye

mackerel sky over
Skye's pure fiction
the Cuillin parallel

sun doesn't rest
on the eye won't sponsor
ultimate journeys:

'e' makes the place halfway
plausible north enough
so Mercator flatters

lends a sense of scale
to triple-rate Skye:
tv and harbour view

hail at the door
the day cut short
as fall ran

spring licked steam
off the ferry deck,
docking slow,

vessel of exchanges
patiently spoken
over bluster tec-

temporal plates
gone: to a takeover
bid syndicating

waterlocked
metabolics
to a standard rate

for fiction a bridge
to empty cottages
of crofters' ghosts.

Leaf-Curling Spider

The eye's blood spot, or else fire licks
above the maple's bed of embers.
A leaf posed in a frozen mid-air trick
fakes zero gravity. It's done with wires.
The leaf curls in around the focal spider,
origamist wormholeing through time
and sapping panic, ever calm insider:
here all future yesterdays must climb
up silk reeled in to where no seconds pass,
the branch forever stripped, the lawn aflame.
The stopper in a fluted hourglass.
The black zero cropped in a crimson frame.
The spider in wait in its conic fold.
The eye in wait behind translucent lid.

Drystone walls

Our hilltop block, steep sloping site,
is terraced with retaining walls.
My chisel breaks cement-work up.

The plan is walls of balanced stone.
I've stocked debris of structures gone,
mere shards, and blocks that must be split,

those wobbling would-be prisms, loaves
squashed out of square in freezer depths,
their pale grain peach-stained,

shiraz splashed. I took whatever
I could get—the neighbour's
knockdown when it crept beyond

the work-site tape—negotiated,
salvaged, thieved. The stones
bore down like thugs onto my back

axle with the chassis tutt-tutt
squealing as the bonnet rose.
My store was listing,

out of true: how to access,
even see, each new
placement's perfect fit?

The plan is walls of balanced stone,
unsealed, retaining soil by art.
Above the block's steep sloping site

I place each stone atop a stone.
Precipitous. Each sloping tier
poised crooked as a backwoods grin

shows more of front than vanity.
All day I fix the terms of truce
with old, stone-savage, gravity.

Afterword

Written mostly over the past four years, the poems in *Rare Bird* look to find what's left when we strip away (or try to strip away) our individual and collective vanities: beneath the sentiment and self-deception, what is pure, or beautiful, or true? These are poems of a sceptic thankful for the inexplicable gift of life.

Many of these poems explore human relationships with the natural world. Others reflect on family, art, and culture, with several poem-essays on art and literature. The final part of the volume becomes increasingly focused on mortality. Collectively the poems enact the elusiveness of moments of connection, communion, and understanding, in the process interrogating the act of writing, its power and severe limitations. These poems insist that Hamlet, Penn and Teller, and Squirrel Nutkin are all fit material for poetry. I've always been suspicious of earnest writing, and believe whimsy often takes us nearer to the truth (thank you John Forbes). This volume invests bullishly in poetic conceits.

The poems also reflect my interest in poetic form. A few years ago I reread Auden and was humbled by his ability to mount sustained and complex arguments (rather than, say, the image-driven emotional lyrics that are so much easier to pull off) within strict metrical forms. An aptly chosen form can, I think, lend an air of inevitability to a poem, a sense of rightness to balance its necessary fragility. The emphatic patterns of repetition that drive a villanelle, the remembered or imagined love (in one form or another) that haunts a sonnet, add to the riskiness and richness of the poem.

Notes

Missing

The poem references Jean-Paul Sartre's *Being and Nothingness* (1943) and its final line reworks the second refrain of Sylvia Plath's villanelle "Mad Girl's Love Song" (1953): 'I think I made you up inside my head.'

Jazz

The Romani-French jazz guitarist Django Reinhardt (1910-1953) had his left hand severely burnt and permanently injured in 1928, but his musical career was unimpeded by this.

The Necklace

This is the title of the story by Guy de Maupassant. The Emile Zola novels referenced are *The Kill, Earth, The Beast Within,* and *Germinal.*

The Lookout Tree

The Notre Dame Cathedral fire of April 2019 is pertinent subtext to this poem.

Fifty

The nominated actors did not (of course) play any of the movie roles attributed to them here, to which they may have been suited.

Song of Innocence

The poem reworks phrases of Stevie Smith's 'Our Bog is Dood' and 'Not Waving but Drowning.' Steve Smith is an Australian cricketer. The scientist and novelist C. P. Snow is best known for his 1959 thesis of 'the two cultures' into which he contends the whole intellectual life of western society is split. John Snow was an English fast bowler of the 1960s and 70s.

Chapel, Port Arthur

This chapel was built as the new Benthamite philosophy of spiritual discipline for prisoners was displacing the older regime of punishment by flogging. At Port Arthur the principle of hierarchy applied even in death, with free settlers' graves on the north side of the Isle of the Dead (facing Home), while convicts were buried on the isle's south side.

Acknowledgements

I'd like to thank the editors of the following publications in which a number of these poems first appeared, sometimes with different titles:

Communion, Cordite Poetry Review, Contrappasso, Heat, Island, New England Poetry Review, Overland, Quadrant, Southerly, and the Henry Kendall Poetry Prize Anthology 2017.

I also thank all those who, at different periods during the past two and a half decades, have read my poems and offered their encouragement and criticism. Thanks especially to Keston Sutherland and John Forbes, to J P Daughton and Jim Provencher, to James Bradley, and to Sarah Newlands, Jonathan Kelt, John Hughes and Luke Harley for their attentive reading of my recent poems. Thank you to Shane Strange at Recent Work Press for bringing this book to publication, and for his judicious suggestions about tweaking the sequence of poems, which have made this a better book. And a final thanks to John Wolseley for generously allowing me to use a detail from his beautifully observed and meditative artwork (an artwork referenced in the title poem) as the cover image.

About the Author

James Lucas was born in Sydney in 1965. He was educated at the University of New South Wales, where he won the University medal, and then Cambridge, where he completed a Ph D in modernist poetry in 1997. He published two chapbooks in the 1990s in the UK, his first Australian poetry publication being in *Southerly* in 1994. Since then his poems have appeared in *Communion, Contrappasso, Cordite Poetry Review, Heat, Island, Meanjin, New England Review, Overland, Quadrant, Salt, Scarp, Southerly*, the Henry Kendall Award Anthology, and the 2020 Newcastle Poetry Prize Anthology. For many years he has taught English at Sydney Grammar School. *Rare Bird* is his first book.

9 780645 008913